Sydney Wood

Sydney Wood has written numerous history books for primary and secondary schools, as well as books and articles for adults. He is a former senior lecturer in history.

Famous People
King Henry VIII
1491–1547

Published by 4Learning
124 Horseferry Road, London SW1P 2TX
Tel: 08701 246 444
www.channel4.com/learning

© 4 Ventures Limited 2003

Written by Sydney Wood

Education Officer: Anne Fleck
Edited and designed by thingswedo
Illustrator: Jacqueline Abrahams
Picture Researcher: Jackie Mace
Printer: ESP Colour
Project Manager: Huw Jones

ISBN 1 86215 989 0

Picture credits

Contents

The new King

On 22 April 1509, Henry became King Henry VIII. Although only 17 years old he was a strong man, 1.80 metres tall, with red hair.

Henry's father, who was also called Henry, had captured the English kingdom for the Tudor family in battle. At Bosworth in 1485 he had beaten and killed the previous King, Richard III. Henry VIII needed to be a good ruler, for he lived in dangerous times.

In June 1509, Henry married Catherine of Aragon, the daughter of the rulers of Spain. On Midsummer Day they were crowned King and Queen at Westminster Abbey in London. Henry walked on a splendid red carpet to enter the Abbey. When he had gone, the crowd tore the carpet to pieces to take home as souvenirs.

Henry was now the most important person in England and Wales. He had been well educated by private tutors and could speak French and Latin as well as English.

Henry became King when he was 17 years old.

For the moment, Henry wanted to enjoy
himself. He loved dancing and feasting, tennis
and archery, and going hunting. Above all,
Henry loved to fight on horseback against
knights in a very dangerous sport called
jousting. Whatever he did, Henry wanted
to be the best at it. He was a vain man
who liked to show off.

Henry wore golden clothes with jewels sewn on and a crimson cloak for his coronation.

Henry's kingdom

Henry was King of England and Wales. He claimed to be Lord of Ireland and King of France too, but Ireland was difficult to control and all he owned in France was the town of Calais. Scotland had its own King, James IV, who married Henry's older sister, Margaret.

Most people in Henry's kingdom lived in the countryside and farmed the land. Families in Tudor times were large. Women usually gave birth to between eight and fifteen children – though at least a quarter died before they became adults. All members of the family had to work. Children as young as seven collected firewood, helped to look after animals and fetched water from wells and streams. The wife and children had to do what the man of the house decided.

The people of Henry's kingdom were all Roman Catholics and the church played a very important part in their lives. Churches were colourful places decorated with pictures and statues of saints and the Holy Family. About 12,000 people gave their lives to God and spent their time in monasteries and nunneries.

In Tudor times, men took animals to market to be sold.

There were around fifty powerful nobles who
were earls, dukes or barons. They controlled
their local areas from castles. The King did not
have a large army of his own. When he needed
an army he called on the nobles to send him
men from their lands. Henry's father had killed
several nobles who were against the Tudor
family, and Henry was careful not to let any
one noble become too powerful.

Children were expected to help their parents make a living.

Life at court

Henry VIII ruled his kingdom himself. He would ask important people for their advice, but he decided what to do. He chose people to help him – and got rid of them as he wished. He had a fierce temper too. People who really angered him were quite likely to be executed.

As many as a thousand people, including about a hundred women, gathered at Henry's court. They included artists, musicians and writers who wanted royal support. The King had many servants too, so his court was a very crowded place. In addition, Henry had many pets such as dogs, ferrets, canaries and nightingales. His wife, Catherine of Aragon, had a pet monkey.

The royal court gathered around the King wherever he chose to live. Henry loved fine palaces. By the end of his reign he owned 55, including Hampton Court, Greenwich Palace and Windsor Castle. He spent a great deal of money on improving his palaces and their gardens.

Cardinal Wolsey was one of King Henry's trusted advisers.

Because Henry liked to spend his time enjoying himself, he needed men to do much of his work for him. For many years he relied on Thomas Wolsey, a butcher's son who had been to Oxford University and became a priest. Wolsey was very clever and eventually became Archbishop of York and a Cardinal – one of the most important people in the Catholic Church. However, Wolsey's wealth and ways angered many nobles. They were pleased when Henry turned against Wolsey and had him arrested. Wolsey died before Henry was able to have him executed.

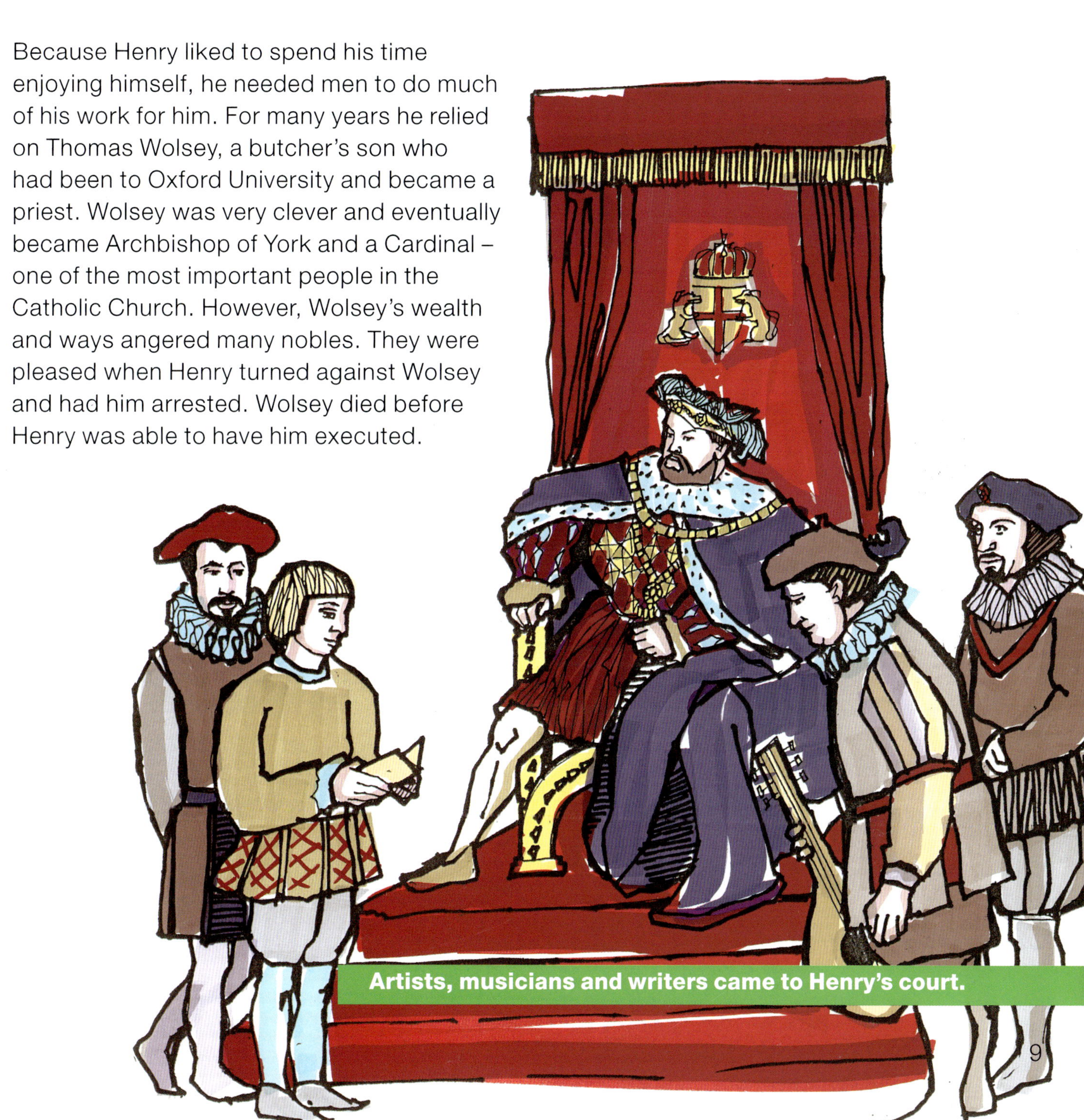

Artists, musicians and writers came to Henry's court.

A warlike King

Henry was keen to win fame through glorious victories. English kings had once ruled a large part of France; now Henry wanted it back. Three times Henry went to war with France. In his first attack in 1513 he won a battle and captured two towns. His later attacks were not so successful.

Henry VIII spent a lot of money on wars.

Henry saw the young King of France, Francis I, as a great rival. In 1520 the two Kings met. Henry challenged Francis to a wrestling match – and was beaten. But he then beat Francis in an archery competition.

France and Scotland were allies. When Henry attacked France, Scottish armies came south to attack England. This led to two terrible defeats for the Scots. The first was at Flodden in 1513 where over 10,000 Scots died including their King, James IV. The second was at Solway Moss in 1542. English soldiers crossed into Scotland and even burned down the city of Edinburgh.

Henry's wars cost a great deal of money. Some of the money went on building new warships. Henry's fleet included the *Great Harry*, which had 184 guns, and the *Mary Rose*, which had 207 guns. In 1545 his fleet drove away a French fleet that was attacking Portsmouth. But the *Mary Rose* sank. Nearly all of its crew of five hundred drowned. The ship lay on the sea bed until 1982 when it was raised.

Henry and Catherine of Aragon

Catherine of Aragon was a popular Queen. She was well educated and very religious. Catherine had six babies. Only her daughter, Mary, was healthy enough to grow up to be an adult. By 1527 it was clear that Catherine, now aged 42, would never have a son.

Henry longed for a son to be King after him. He believed England needed a man to rule in troubled times. Henry grew tired of Catherine and fell in love with Anne Boleyn, who was ten years younger than him. He longed to leave Catherine and marry Anne. But the Pope and the Catholic Church had rules that made divorce very difficult indeed.

Henry tried to persuade the Pope that his marriage to Catherine had been wrong. When this did not work, Henry called a meeting of Parliament. It agreed to pass a law stating that the King of England, not the Pope, was in overall charge of the English Church. This meant that Henry was now able to divorce Catherine and marry Anne.

In January 1533 Henry secretly married Anne Boleyn. Then Thomas Cranmer, a clergyman, declared Henry's marriage to Catherine had never been a proper marriage, but that he was truly married to Anne. Anne was crowned Queen. Catherine lived under house arrest in great unhappiness. She died in 1536. Her last words were about Henry – 'Mine eyes desire you above all things.'

Thomas Cranmer helped Henry end his marriage to Catherine.

The break with Rome

Many men in Parliament did not like the great power of the Catholic Church. In 1534 a law declared that Henry, not the Pope, was now the Supreme Head of the Church in England. The Pope was furious. He declared Henry was no longer a member of the Catholic Church.

A growing number of people wanted even more change. They supported the ideas of a German monk called Martin Luther. He attacked many of the Catholic Church's beliefs. It is said that Luther wrote out his complaints and nailed them to the door of a church. He believed that the Pope was too powerful. He also believed that priests should not be so important and that ordinary people should pray directly to God. At first, Henry opposed Luther. He even wrote a book attacking him. But soon Henry realised that he and Luther were both enemies of the Pope.

Martin Luther was a Protestant.

William Tyndale translated the Bible into English.

William Tyndale, an Englishman who lived in Germany, also supported Luther's ideas. He began to write out the Bible in English. Until now, the Bible had been in Latin, which only priests and educated people could read. Henry tried to stop Tyndale's Bible entering England. But in 1537 two of the King's advisers, Thomas Cromwell and Thomas Cranmer, persuaded Henry to allow a Bible in English to be placed in every church.

Henry demanded that all clergymen and the most important men in England accept that he was now head of the Church. Some clergy who refused were put in prison. Bishop Fisher and Sir Thomas More both refused. The two men were beheaded in 1535.

Queen Anne – but not for long

Anne Boleyn became Queen in 1533. Henry had left the wife he had been married to for over twenty years for Anne. But three years later Anne was dead. Henry, her husband, had ordered her execution. So what went wrong?

Henry's second wife was a very clever, lively, well-educated person. She was very interested in religion and in all that happened in the world. But Anne made fun of Henry in front of other people. She argued with him and made jokes about his clothes and the poetry he wrote. The King did not like this. Anne had given birth to a daughter, Elizabeth, in 1533, but Henry longed for a wife who might give him a son. He turned to other women and a plot began against Anne.

Anne Boleyn was executed at the Tower of London.

Anne had many enemies. Thomas Cromwell organised them and gathered evidence against Anne. Several people agreed to say that she had affairs with other men. They said that the Queen planned to kill the King and marry one of them. The Queen's musician, Mark Smeaton, was tortured. He was tied to a machine that pulled his body apart until he agreed he was guilty of having an affair with Anne. All this evidence was probably false, but Henry believed it.

Five men said to have had affairs with Anne, plus the Queen herself, were seized and locked in the Tower of London. At their trial they were all found guilty. This meant they were all executed. Anne wore a black dress for her execution and faced her death very bravely.

Henry VIII loved colourful clothes.

17

A son at last

King Henry VIII's son, Edward

Less than two weeks after Anne Boleyn's death, Henry married again. His new wife was 27-year-old Jane Seymour. Jane was quiet, sensible and believed that a wife should obey her husband. Jane helped to bring together the King and Princess Mary, the daughter he had with Catherine of Aragon.

On 12 October 1537 Jane gave birth to a baby boy. Henry wept tears of joy when he first held his son. All over England, church bells rang out. The cannon at the Tower of London fired 2,000 times in celebration. The baby was born and christened with the name Edward at Hampton Court, one of Henry's many palaces.

The King spent £62,000 (equal to about £19m today) on improving Hampton Court and its gardens. But even this, and his many other palaces, was not enough for Henry. In 1538, 520 workmen began building Nonsuch Palace. Henry meant it to be the finest palace in Europe. When he died, £24,000 (over £7m) had been spent on it.

The King's joy soon turned to sadness. Twelve days after giving birth to Edward, Jane died of blood poisoning. She was the only one of Henry's wives to be buried as Queen. Many women died after childbirth. Doctors were not well educated and could not cure most illnesses. When a terrible illness (like plague) appeared anywhere in England, Henry went to live as far away from it as possible.

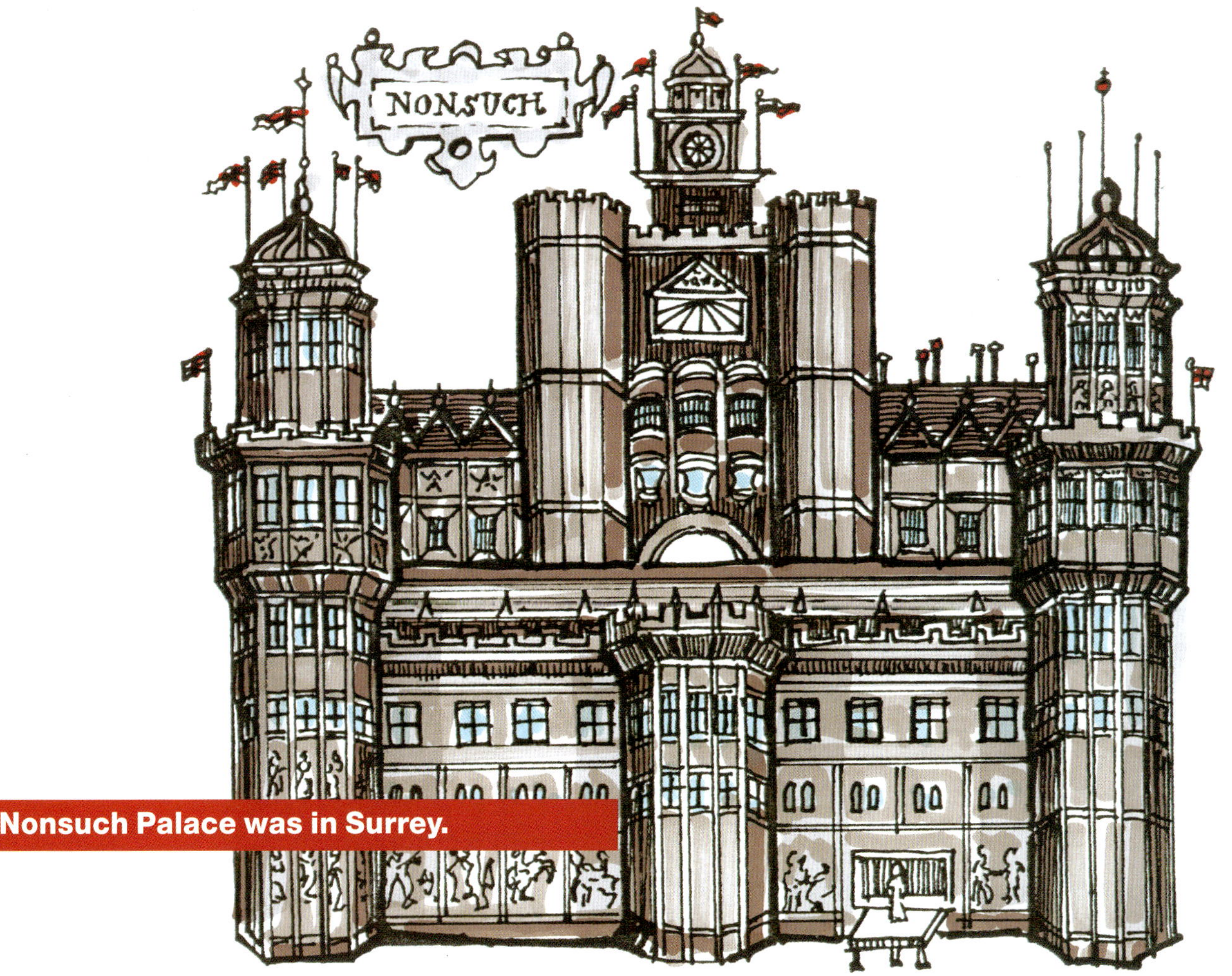

Nonsuch Palace was in Surrey.

19

Destroy the monasteries

Henry needed money for his expensive life and for his wars. His idea was to close all the monasteries and raise money by selling their land. Cromwell sent men to visit monasteries to prove that they ought to be closed.

Many people did not want the monasteries closed. Monks and nuns cared for the sick and looked after travellers. Some monks and nuns did not behave as they should, but Cromwell's report made it sound as if all monasteries should be closed because they were run by dishonest people. Henry was pleased and ordered that it should be done.

The Pilgrimage of Grace (1536) was the name given to the great uprising of people in the north of England against the closing of monasteries. There were so many thousands of angry people that the King had to send the Duke of Norfolk to meet their leader, Robert Aske. The Duke promised that Parliament would meet to discuss their demands. But when Henry sent armies north, they seized many men and hanged them. Robert Aske was executed.

Warden Abbey in Bedfordshire, once a monastery, is now a house.

Bayham Abbey in Kent used to be a monastery.

By 1540 the monasteries had all gone. Henry took all of their gold and silver objects as well as their jewels. He kept some of the monasteries' lands, gave some land to rich friends and sold off the rest. Monks who agreed to go peacefully were given very small pensions. Monks who opposed the King were imprisoned or hanged. Now Henry was rich again.

A six-month long marriage

In 1540 Thomas Cromwell was made Earl of Essex. He was a powerful man and persuaded the King to marry Anne of Cleves. The artist Holbein went to Cleves in Germany to paint a picture of Anne. Henry liked it. But when Henry met Anne in person he disliked her at once.

Henry tried to avoid marrying Anne but the wedding went ahead. He blamed Cromwell. Henry had fallen in love with Catherine Howard and wanted his marriage to Anne to end. Catherine's uncle, the Duke of Norfolk, hated Cromwell. He found people ready to say that Cromwell was a traitor who did not agree with the King's religious ideas but preferred Luther's instead. Cromwell was arrested and executed on 28 July 1540.

Henry's officials gathered reasons to prove that the King's marriage to Anne had not been legal. The Church and Parliament agreed. Anne did not argue when she was told her marriage was over. She lived happily in a palace that Henry gave her until she died in 1557.

Henry decided to meet Anne of Cleves when he was shown a portrait of her.

Holbein's portrait of Anne of Cleves

A wife – who can't be trusted

Henry loved eating and drinking.

On the day that Cromwell died, Henry married again. His new wife, Catherine Howard, was not a highly educated or very serious girl. She wanted to enjoy herself and had several lovers. Her music teacher, Henry Mannock, loved her but Catherine left him and began an affair with Francis Dereham, a handsome young gentleman.

Catherine joined the royal court. She began an affair with Thomas Culpeper, one of the King's favourites. But once Henry met Catherine, her other men friends were pushed aside, for the King fell in love with her. Aged 49, Henry was 29 years older than Catherine. He loved eating and drinking so much that he was becoming fat. Still, Catherine loved the idea of being Queen and married Henry. He gave her anything she wanted – jewels, clothes, even lands that had once been Cromwell's.

The Howard family, to which Catherine belonged, had enemies including Thomas Cranmer, Archbishop of Canterbury, and Edward, Jane Seymour's brother. These men supported Luther's 'Protestant' ideas. They disliked the Howard family's power and their Catholic beliefs.

In October 1541 Mary Hall, a servant to Catherine's uncle, the Duke of Norfolk, told her brother, John Lascelles, about Catherine's early affairs. John knew Cranmer and told him. Catherine's enemies then learned that she was seeing Culpeper, secretly. They found a letter in which Catherine declared how much she cared for Culpeper. When Cranmer gave Henry a note listing his wife's affairs, the King refused to believe it. He wept, then full of rage had everyone involved arrested and executed – including Catherine.

Catherine Howard was the second of Henry's wives to be executed.

Catherine Parr and Henry's last years

On 12 July 1543, Henry married again. Catherine Parr was 31 years old and had been married twice already – both of her husbands had died. Catherine was a quiet, sensible, thoughtful and well-educated lady. Like Henry, she enjoyed music and she knew French, Italian and Latin. She was very loyal to Henry and did not argue with him. She kept greyhounds and parrots as pets.

Catherine soon became a good friend of Henry's daughter, Mary. Princess Elizabeth had been left very much on her own. Catherine brought Elizabeth to court and gave her rooms near her own. She made sure Elizabeth was properly educated. Prince Edward, too, became very fond of the Queen.

Catherine Parr was Henry's sixth and final wi[fe]

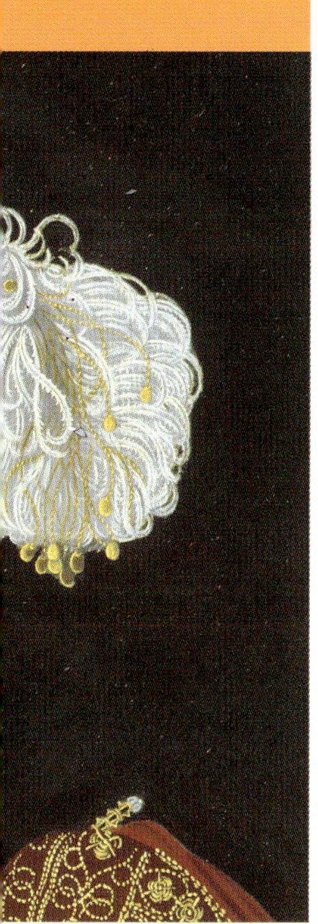

Catherine was very interested in Protestant religious beliefs. The Duke of Norfolk and his son hated Protestant ideas and they tried to ruin Catherine. Anne Askew, a Protestant lady, was tortured on the rack in the hope that she would say the Queen agreed with her religious beliefs. But Anne would not confess and was burned to death as a heretic. The Queen was safe.

Henry was now fatter than ever. He had to be carried everywhere on a specially made chair covered in velvet cloth. He was lifted up stairs and onto his bed with ropes and pulleys. The King's temper was worse than ever. Catherine nursed the King until he died on 28 January 1547. Catherine died the following year.

Henry VIII with Jane Seymour and his three children: Mary, Elizabeth and Edward.

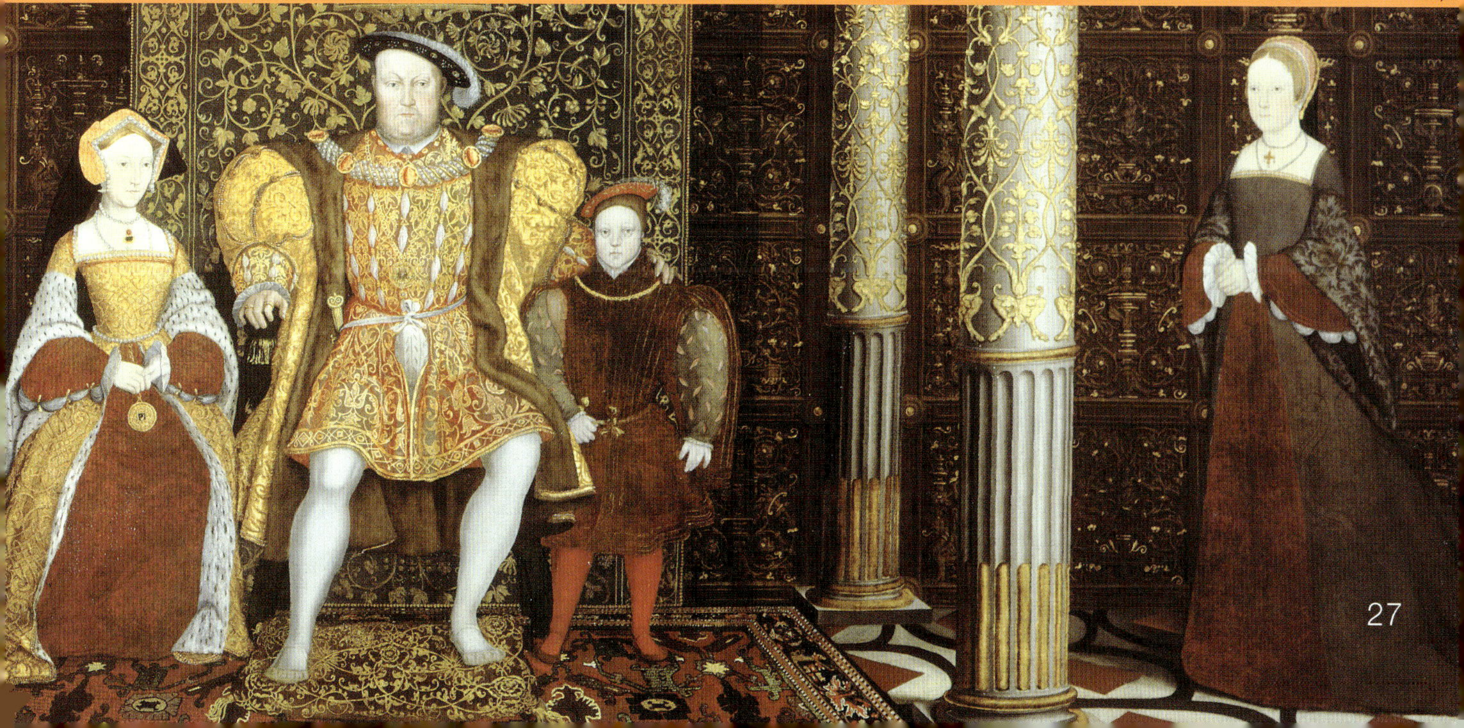

A timeline of Henry VIII's life

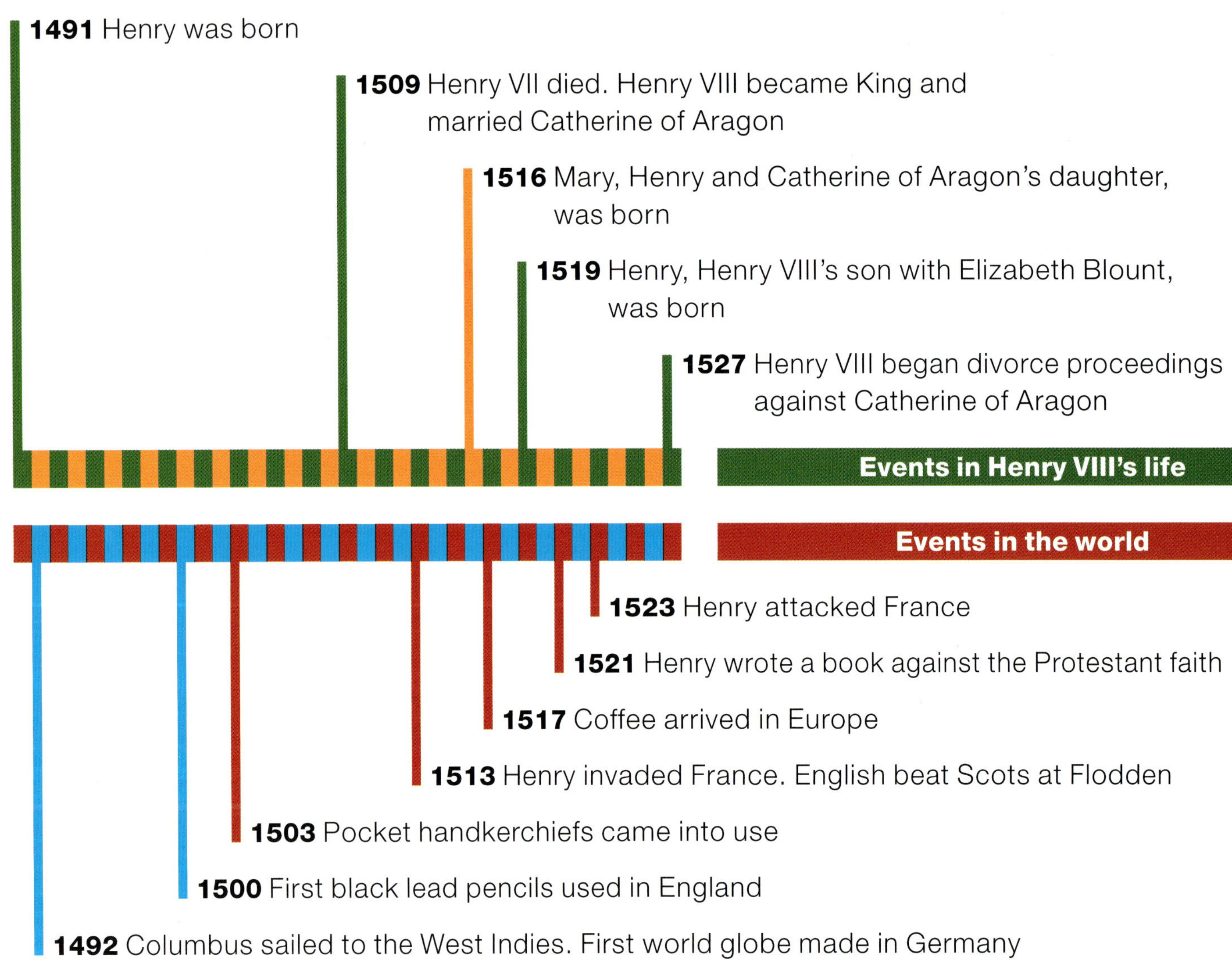

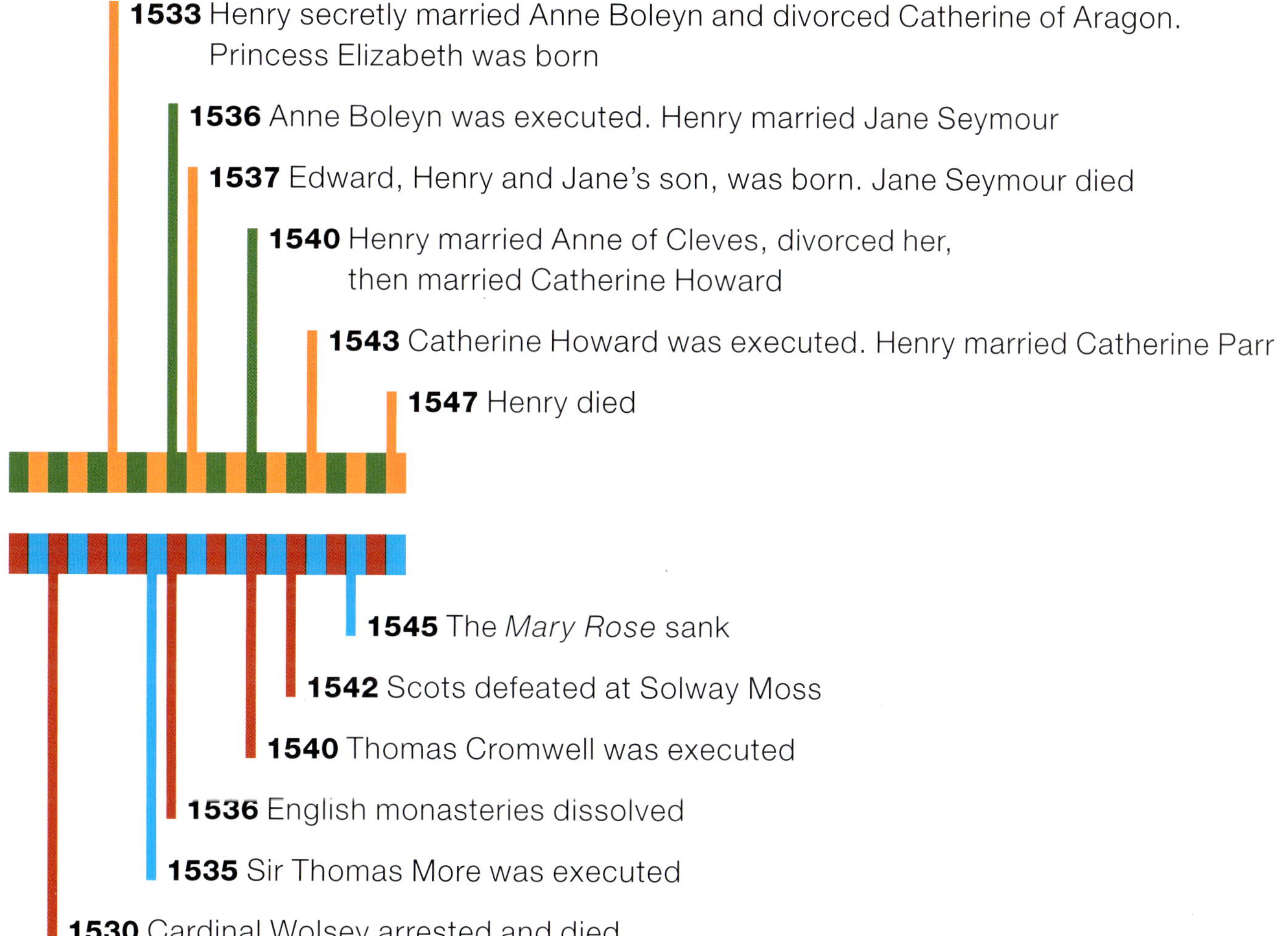

1533 Henry secretly married Anne Boleyn and divorced Catherine of Aragon. Princess Elizabeth was born
1536 Anne Boleyn was executed. Henry married Jane Seymour
1537 Edward, Henry and Jane's son, was born. Jane Seymour died
1540 Henry married Anne of Cleves, divorced her, then married Catherine Howard
1543 Catherine Howard was executed. Henry married Catherine Parr
1547 Henry died
1545 The Mary Rose sank
1542 Scots defeated at Solway Moss
1540 Thomas Cromwell was executed
1536 English monasteries dissolved
1535 Sir Thomas More was executed
1530 Cardinal Wolsey arrested and died

Henry's family tree

Henry VIII

m 1509   *m 1533*   *m 1536*   *m 1540*   *m 1540*   *m 1543*

Catherine of Aragon

Anne Boleyn

Jane Seymour

Anne of Cleves

Catherine Howard

Catherine Parr

Mary Tudor

Elizabeth I

Edward VI

Glossary

archery *(5)* Shooting with a bow and arrow.

Catholic *(6)* Someone who believes that the Pope is head of the Church.

divorce *(12)* The ending of a marriage by law.

fleet *(11)* A group of ships sailing together.

heretic *(27)* Someone with a religious belief that is very different from the belief that is generally accepted.

jousting *(5)* A sport in which people on horseback fight against each other using a long weapon called a lance.

Latin *(4)* The language spoken by the Romans.

monasteries *(6)* Buildings in which men live according to strict religious rules.

nunneries *(6)* Buildings in which women live according to strict religious rules.

parliament *(13)* A group of people who represent a country.

pension *(21)* A regular payment to someone who has retired from work.

plague *(19)* A terrible disease causing fever and often death.

Pope *(12)* Head of the Catholic Church.

Protestant *(14)* Someone who believes that the Pope is not head of the Church.

souvenir *(4)* An object that recalls a certain place or occasion.

torture *(17)* Causing extreme pain to someone to make them do or say something.

traitor *(22)* Someone who betrays another person or persons, or their country.

Index

More books to read

Henry VIII and His Six Wives by John Guy (Ticktock Media, 1995)

The Reign of Henry VIII: Personalities and Politics by David Starkey (Vintage, 2002)

Henry VIII: King and Court by Alison Weir (Pimlico, 2002)